ANOINTING

SCRIPTURES & PRAYERS TO
R E L E A S E
G O D ' S   P O W E R
I N   Y O U R   L I F E

JOSHUA MILLS

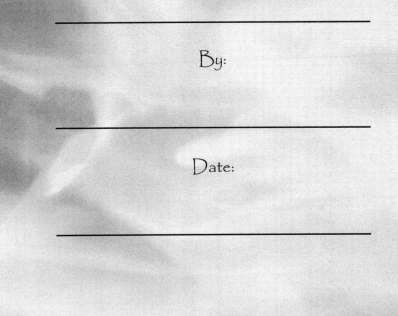

This Book Is Presented To:

_____

By:

_____

Date:

_____

The ANOINTING

SCRIPTURES & PRAYERS TO
R E L E A S E
G O D ' S   P O W E R
I N   Y O U R   L I F E

JOSHUA MILLS

**International Glory Ministries
P.O. Box 4037
Palm Springs, CA 92263
JoshuaMills.com
info@joshuamills.com**

Published by New Wine International, Inc
Editing and layout by Harold McDougal
Cover design by Ken Vail

ISBN: 978-1-61917-011-7

Printed in the United States of America

Dedication

This book is dedicated to every hungry and thirsty believer who desires to move in a greater flow of God's power. The anointing is available and accessible for all those who believe!

Introduction

...the Spirit of the LORD will come powerfully upon you, and you will prophesy with them. You will be changed into a different person.
– 1 Samuel 10:6, NLT

When the fresh anointing of God's Spirit begins to fill your life, something very powerful begins to happen, and you *will* be changed. Every moment of anointing is a moment of change.

In writing this book of affirmations, scriptures, and prayers concerning the anointing of God's Spirit, my desire is for each and every reader to have their own dramatic encounters with the power of God—life-changing, transforming, world-shaking, never-the-same-again encounters that ignite such a flame inside of you that you'll become an anointed carrier of His revival fire and will set your world ablaze for Jesus!

The key here is that you must allow the Spirit of the Lord to come powerfully upon you. This will require the sacrifice of your time, your passionate pursuit, and your willingness to agree with the Word of God in yielded surrender.

One of the ways I've personally learned how to come into deeper encounters with God is by focusing on His truths and allowing them to sink deep within my spirit, until I can speak them out loud from my heart with genuine conviction. This book is an invitation for you to do the same.

In this book, I've compiled scriptures about the anointing, along with personal prayers and affirmations that will help connect you to a new anointing. As you read them and pray them aloud over your personal life, home, family, business, ministry, and region, allow the Spirit to lead you through the pages. May you experience revival fire and the oil of His presence as you discover the power of *The ANOINTING*.

Joshua Mills

The place of my dwelling is anointed!

*So early in the morning Jacob took
the stone that he had put under
his head and set it up for a pillar
and poured oil on the top of it.*
– Genesis 28:18

ANOINTING

Father, in the name of Jesus, I dedicate myself and the place of my dwelling to be used by Your Spirit to bring honor to Your name. Thank You for Your anointing that is present wherever I happen to lay my head. Let me be anointed this day for Your divine purposes. Use me and my surroundings to build Your Kingdom in the hearts of men and women everywhere.

I am in covenant with the God of the Universe, and I go forth in His name!

I am the God of Bethel, where you anointed a pillar and made a vow to me. Now arise, go out from this land and return to the land of your kindred.
– Genesis 31:13

The ANOINTING

Father, in the name of Jesus, I, too, have made a vow to You. I have submitted myself to You—body, soul, and spirit. You are my God, and I am Your child. Therefore, I stand eager and ready to be sent wherever You need me in Your great harvest field. Let Your anointed will for me today be made clear, and I will arise and go in Your name.

My heart is moved to contribute of what I have, that God's power might be known throughout the whole earth!

The LORD said to Moses, "Speak to the people of Israel, that they take for me a contribution. From every man whose heart moves him you shall receive the contribution for me. And this is the contribution that you shall receive from them: gold, silver, and bronze, blue and purple and scarlet yarns and fine twined linen, goats' hair, tanned rams' skins, goatskins, acacia wood."
– Exodus 25:1-5

The ANOINTING

Father, in the name of Jesus, my heart is moved, and I offer myself to You today as a vessel to flow with Your anointing. I am also moved to offer a contribution of what I have. Anything and everything I own I lay at Your feet. Anoint me for Your purposes and lead me in the way You would have me to go, that You might be exalted in all that I do and say.

I am anointed with fresh oil and
carry the fragrance of heaven!

*Oil for the lamps, spices for
the anointing oil and for
the fragrant incense.*

– Exodus 25:6

The ANOINTING

Father, in the name of Jesus, thank You for the oil of Your Spirit that changes me and prepares me for service. Let Your divine fragrance so permeate my being that everyone I meet is affected. Anoint everything I touch for Your glory. I want to live my life so that those around me can always sense Your anointing in me.

I have oil in my lamp, and
it continually burns!

*You shall command the people of
Israel that they bring to you pure
beaten olive oil for the light, that a
lamp may regularly be set up to burn.*

– Exodus 27:20

The ANOINTING

Father, in the name of Jesus, thank You for the light of Your Holy Spirit. I no longer stumble in darkness. Therefore, through You, I now dedicate myself to be the light of this world. Let the oil of Your Spirit increase in my life more and more, so that my lamp never goes out. Let Your light shine on me, in me, and through me.

I am anointed to serve!

And you shall put them on Aaron your brother, and on his sons with him, and shall anoint them and ordain them and consecrate them, that they may serve me as priests.
– Exodus 28:41

The ANOINTING

Father, in the name of Jesus, what a privilege it is to be called Your child, and what a privilege it is to serve You! May I be anointed for everything I attempt to do in Your service. I want to honor You in every way and to be a worthy servant in all that I do and say.

The oil of God's anointing has been poured over me so that everything I do is blessed!

You shall take the anointing oil and pour it on his head and anoint him.
– Exodus 29:7

The ANOINTING

Father, in the name of Jesus, thank You for the oil of Your Spirit that pours down upon me. My desire is to live in that anointing every moment of every day. Nothing could give me more pleasure. This anointing, I realize, has a purpose, and I dedicate myself fully to Your purposes. Let Your supernatural anointing oil flow through me with unlimited blessing.

The anointing of God's Spirit is not only changing my own life; it is also impacting all those around me!

The holy garments of Aaron shall be for his sons after him; they shall be anointed in them and ordained in them.
– Exodus 29:29

The ANOINTING

Father, in the name of Jesus, thank You that Your blessings are not just for me, but for all those that concern me. Be magnified in my spiritual children, my spiritual grandchildren and all those who come after me. Let Your anointing set apart each generation as holy unto You.

I love the anointing of God's Spirit,
for it changes everything!

*And you shall make of these a
sacred anointing oil blended
as by the perfumer; it shall
be a holy anointing oil.*
– Exodus 30:25

The ANOINTING

Father, in the name of Jesus, thank You for the holy anointing oil that is still flowing to us today in the twenty-first century. I believe You are the same yesterday, today, and forever. Let the power of Your anointing rest upon me today, so that the world may see and know that You are available to those who sincerely seek You.

God's anointing is with me as I glorify Him, as I sing praises to Him, and I allow His Spirit to work in me!

With it you shall anoint the tent of meeting and the ark of the testimony.
— Exodus 30:26

The ANOINTING

Father, in the name of Jesus, thank You for the privilege of gathering with Your children everywhere. When we get together, Your presence is with us in unusual ways. You speak to us, You do miracles among us, and You change us for Your glory. Teach me to walk in the power of Your Spirit, that Your Kingdom may be established more fully in my life and in the lives of all those I touch.

I will not accept any substitute for
the anointing of the Spirit!

*And you shall say to the people
of Israel, "This shall be my
holy anointing oil throughout
your generations."*
– Exodus 30:31

The ANOINTING

Father, in the name of Jesus, You have provided a miraculous anointing for us in our time, preparing us and equipping us for daily living, for interaction with those around us, and for service in Your Church. Why would we accept any substitute? We welcome You to continue to work in our lives every moment of every day. In all that we do and say, we desire to honor You, as we walk in the anointing of Your Spirit.

I stand in awe of the anointing of God's power; in a moment's time, He does what no man could ever do!

It shall not be poured on the body of an ordinary person, and you shall make no other like it in composition. It is holy, and it shall be holy to you. Whoever compounds any like it or whoever puts any of it on an outsider shall be cut off from his people.
— Exodus 30:32-33

The ANOINTING

Father, in the name of Jesus, I am wholly dependent upon Your Spirit for life and breath, but also for wisdom, knowledge, and understanding. Without Your touch, I am nothing and have nothing to offer to others. In You, I find completion and expansion and can extend the blessing over my life to those around me. Thank You, Holy God of power and might.

Nothing can compare with what
the anointing does in my life!

*He made the holy anointing oil
also, and the pure fragrant incense,
blended as by the perfumer.*
– Exodus 37:29

The ANOINTING

Father, in the name of Jesus, I delight in the excellence of Your holy anointing and find in it all that I need for life in the here and now. You fill me, thrill me, and overflow me. May the fragrance of Your Holy Spirit flow forth from my life to bless others everywhere I go.

I am determined that everything, even the most insignificant things in my daily life, will be anointed for God's glory!

Then you shall take the anointing oil and anoint the tabernacle and all that is in it, and consecrate it and all its furniture, so that it may become holy.
– Exodus 40:9

The ANOINTING

Father, in the name of Jesus, I thank You that You are willing and desirous of being involved in the smallest details of my life. Your love fills my heart and overflows into every other part of me like warm, flowing oil, that brings comfort, joy, healing and peace. I give You Lordship over every decision, every action, and every reaction that I make. May You be seen as the Anointed One in me.

I am anointed to minister!

And put on Aaron the holy garments. And you shall anoint him and consecrate him, that he may serve me as priest. You shall bring his sons also and put coats on them, and anoint them, as you anointed their father, that they may serve me as priests. And their anointing shall admit them to a perpetual priesthood throughout their generations.
– Exodus 40:13-15

The ANOINTING

Father, in the name of Jesus, thank You for the privilege of serving You. You have not only called me; You have also equipped me through the anointing and gifts of Your Holy Spirit. May I be anointed in all that I do, that Your love and power might be demonstrated through me toward others.

I dedicate myself to the purity
of God's anointing!

*If it is the anointed priest who
sins, thus bringing guilt on the
people, then he shall offer for the
sin that he has committed a bull
from the herd without blemish
to the LORD for a sin offering.*
– Leviticus 4:3

The ANOINTING

Father, in the name of Jesus, thank You for the privilege of representing You to my family, friends, neighbors, and fellow co-workers in the Kingdom. Help me to be worthy of that calling and to bear with honor Your sacred touch upon my life. Thank You for purifying me by the flame of Your Spirit, as I humble myself before You as a living sacrifice of pure worship. I desire to walk in Your anointing with holiness.

I am the temple of the Holy Spirit,
and this temple is anointed!

*Then Moses took the anointing oil
and anointed the tabernacle and all
that was in it, and consecrated them.*
– Leviticus 8:10

The ANOINTING

Father, in the name of Jesus, thank You for the privilege of being the temple of Your Holy Spirit. I do not take this privilege lightly. I invite You to work through me in greater ways, that others may be blessed, and Your name may be exalted.

I am fully consecrated to the
Lord and His work!

*And he sprinkled some of it on the
altar seven times, and anointed the
altar and all its utensils and the basin
and its stand, to consecrate them.*
– Leviticus 8:11

The ANOINTING

Father, in the name of Jesus, I am Yours. I give You permission to do with me as You will. I know that Your ways are always best, so I rest in the assurance that allowing You to have control insures that I am guided along the right path and perfectly directed into Your anointed plan for my life.

19

My head is anointed!

And he poured some of the anointing oil on Aaron's head and anointed him to consecrate him.
– Leviticus 8:12

The ANOINTING

Father, in the name of Jesus, I ask You to anoint my head more and more, that I might think Your thoughts, understand Your ways, and be able to walk in that which pleases You every hour of every day. Let Your holy oil drip down from the top of my head and cover me completely with a fresh anointing.

20

My whole life is anointed!

Then Moses took some of the anointing oil and of the blood that was on the altar and sprinkled it on Aaron and his garments, and also on his sons and his sons' garments. So he consecrated Aaron and his garments, and his sons and his sons' garments with him.
– Leviticus 8:30

The ANOINTING

Father, in the name of Jesus, how I rejoice that You have anointed every area of my life! I love You and desire to see Your name exalted in every sphere of my influence. Use me in any way You see fit. Continue to anoint all of my personal portals—my heart, my mouth, my eyes and ears, my mind, my innermost being, my hands and feet. I want my every action to bring You honor and praise.

21

I am determined to live in the
holiness of God's light!

*And the priest who is anointed
and consecrated as priest in his
father's place shall make atonement,
wearing the holy linen garments.*
– Leviticus 16:32

The ANOINTING

Father, in the name of Jesus, holiness belongs to You and You alone. Only You are holy. Through the anointing of Your Spirit, let a touch of Your holiness rest upon me this day. May I overcome all my fleshly tendencies, to live and walk in the realm of Your Spirit.

22

I am a releaser of God's holy anointing!

And Eleazar the son of Aaron the priest shall have charge of the oil for the light, the fragrant incense, the regular grain offering, and the anointing oil, with the oversight of the whole tabernacle and all that is in it, of the sanctuary and its vessels.
– Numbers 4:16

The ANOINTING

Father, in the name of Jesus, I delight in Your holy presence. Let the residue of heaven be upon me as I go about my daily activities. May I be anointed for even the most simple of tasks. May the natural of my life become supernatural, for Your honor and glory.

23

I am lifted and qualified
through the anointing!

*The trees once went out to anoint
a king over them, and they said to
the olive tree, "Reign over us."*
– Judges 9:8

The ANOINTING

Father, in the name of Jesus, I daily recognize my nothingness without You, but I also recognize my "everythingness" with, in, and through You. Your anointing makes all the difference. With Your powerful touch on my life, I can conquer every giant that opposes the work of Your anointing.

24

I am anointed to do what is expected
of me this day and every day!

*And the bramble said to the trees,
"If in good faith you are anointing
me king over you, then come and
take refuge in my shade, but if not,
let fire come out of the bramble and
devour the cedars of Lebanon."*
– Judges 9:15

The ANOINTING

Father, in the name of Jesus, I stand in Your power and know without a doubt that I can handle whatever comes my way this day. You have granted me the privilege of serving in Your Kingdom, and have anointed me for whatever I will face. Anoint my entire world this day for the glory of Your name.

25

I am washed, I am anointed, I am ready
for what God is doing in my life!

Wash therefore and anoint yourself,
and put on your cloak and go down to
the threshing floor, but do not make
yourself known to the man until he
has finished eating and drinking.
– Ruth 3:3

The ANOINTING

Father, in the name of Jesus, what I see in the Spirit excites me. You have great plans for my life. If there are other things I need to do to prepare for what is ahead, show me. I desire to do Your will. Let heavenly instruction come to me daily through Your Spirit.

I am anointed for a divine purpose!

*Tomorrow about this time I will
send to you a man from the land
of Benjamin, and you shall anoint
him to be prince over my people
Israel. He shall save my people
from the hand of the Philistines.
For I have seen my people, because
their cry has come to me.*
— 1 Samuel 9:16

The ANOINTING

Father, in the name of Jesus, I have seen in part what You have planned, and I want to know more. I sense that I cannot afford to waste a single day, and I cannot afford to be distracted by the enemy's stalling tactics. Since my life is to count for eternity and to affect others along the way, help me to make the best of every day.

27

> I choose to live in
> the anointed will of God!

Then Samuel took a flask of oil and poured it on his head and kissed him and said, "Has not the LORD anointed you to be prince over his people Israel? And you shall reign over the people of the LORD and you will save them from the hand of their surrounding enemies. And this shall be the sign to you that the LORD has anointed you to be prince over his heritage."
– 1 Samuel 10:1

The ANOINTING

Father, in the name of Jesus, I say, "Not my will, but Yours be done." My insight is so limited, but Yours is not. My strength is limited, but Yours is not. Help me to live this day in Your strength and from Your divine perspective.

28

I am anointed in *"the rush"* of the Spirit!

Then Samuel took the horn of oil and anointed him in the midst of his brothers. And the Spirit of the LORD rushed upon David from that day forward.
— 1 Samuel 16:13

The Anointing

Father, in the name of Jesus, when Your Spirit rushes upon me, I sense that it is for an eternal purpose. You are using me for Your honor and glory, for the upbuilding of Your Kingdom, and I am overwhelmed with gratitude. Anoint me more and more as I yield to the movement of Your Spirit.

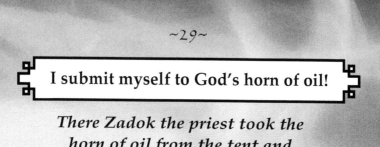

29

I submit myself to God's horn of oil!

There Zadok the priest took the horn of oil from the tent and anointed Solomon. Then they blew the trumpet, and all the people said, "Long live King Solomon!"
– 1 Kings 1:39

The ANOINTING

Father, in the name of Jesus, I feel Your horn of oil pouring down on me even now. Show me what my role is to be this day. I will be careful to walk in Your presence and maintain Your anointing upon my life.

30

I honor, acknowledge, and
uplift God's anointed ones!

*And Jehu the son of Nimshi you
shall anoint to be king over Israel,
and Elisha the son of Shaphat of
Abel-meholah you shall anoint
to be prophet in your place.*
– 1 Kings 19:16

The ANOINTING

Father, in the name of Jesus, thank You for Your care of me personally. Thank You also for Your concern for those around me who hunger and thirst for righteousness. I sense that You would have me to influence them with all that I do and say. Help me to be the best influence I can be in every way.

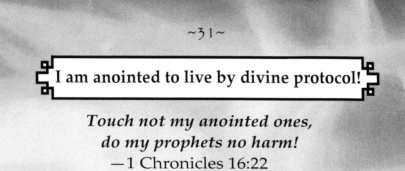

31

I am anointed to live by divine protocol!

Touch not my anointed ones,
do my prophets no harm!
—1 Chronicles 16:22

The ANOINTING

Father, in the name of Jesus, You are Lord over Your Church, and You are Lord over my life. Help me to respect and honor all those whom You have chosen, equipped, and placed in position of leadership over and among Your people. Because they are Yours, I recognize Your touch on their lives and will do whatever I can to be a blessing to them and their call!

32

I can overcome in the anointing
and its protection for my life!

*The kings of the earth set
themselves, and the rulers take
counsel together, against the
LORD and against his Anointed.*
– Psalm 2:2

The ANOINTING

Father, in the name of Jesus, men who do not know You often hate You and work to defeat Your purposes. You taught us that as they persecuted Your Son Jesus, they would also persecute us. Grant me the proper perspective toward such men and women, that I might love my enemies, bless those who curse me, do good to those who hate me, and pray for those who despitefully use me and persecute me.

33

I am protected by the anointing of God's Spirit today and forever!

Now I know that the LORD saves his anointed; he will answer him from his holy heaven with the saving might of his right hand.
– Psalm 20:6

The ANOINTING

Father, in the name of Jesus, the saving power of Your right hand has not diminished with the passage of time. As You were with Moses and Joshua, as You were with David and Solomon, and as You were with Paul and Silas, so You are with me this day. Your right hand shields and protects me.

34

I am overflowing in the anointing!

The LORD is my shepherd; I shall not want. He makes me lie down in green pastures. He leads me beside still waters. He restores my soul. ... Your rod and your staff, they comfort me. You prepare a table before me in the presence of my enemies; you anoint my head with oil; my cup overflows.

– Psalm 23:1-5

The ANOINTING

Father, in the name of Jesus, You are my Overflow. I choose to follow the anointing of Your Spirit, because I know I cannot go wrong when I do. As You open new spiritual pathways before me to walk in, I will be sensitive to recognize them and to follow Your leading. I know that You love me and only lead me into what is best for my life. Therefore I will gladly walk in Your light and allow You to shine in and through my life every day.

35

I am joyfully anointed for
divine supernatural works!

You have loved righteousness and
hated wickedness. Therefore God, your
God, has anointed you with the oil of
gladness beyond your companions.
– Psalm 45:7

The ANOINTING

Father, in the name of Jesus, I bow before You today, recognizing Your greatness. Even as You clothed Your Son with the oil of gladness, You have invited us to share in that same Spirit. You have said that if we believe, we can do the same works as Jesus and even greater works. Let this day be the beginning of the greater works in my life through the precious oil of Your anointing.

36

I can do exploits because of the
anointing that rests upon my life!

*I have found David, my servant; with
my holy oil I have anointed him.*
– Psalm 89:20

The ANOINTING

Father, in the name of Jesus, as I read of the exploits of Your people down through the ages, it is not just history for me. For me, it is a wonderful challenge. If the same Spirit that rested upon them, causing them to defeat giants, conquer lands, and establish Your will on the physical earth, now rests upon me, I can do the impossible today and every day. And I will!

37

I live in the bliss of God's
powerful presence!

*And wine to gladden the heart of
man, oil to make his face shine and
bread to strengthen man's heart.*
– Psalm 104:15

The ANOINTING

Father, in the name of Jesus, You are the joy of my life. The wine of Your Spirit gladdens my heart, the oil of Your Spirit makes my face shine, and the miracle manna of Your Spirit strengthens my heart. Nothing could be more wonderful!

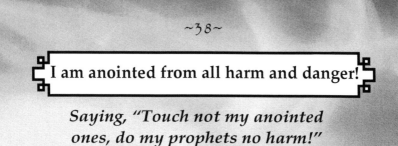

~38~

I am anointed from all harm and danger!

Saying, "Touch not my anointed ones, do my prophets no harm!"
– Psalm 105:15

The ANOINTING

Father, in the name of Jesus, You are a Shield about me, my Glory, and the Lifter of my head. When I cry out to You, You hear me from Your holy hill and answer. When I lie down, I am able to sleep, for You sustain me. I awake refreshed and invigorated and ready for every new challenge. To You be all the praise!

39

I am living in the oil of unity, and will do everything to protect it!

Behold, how good and pleasant it is when brothers dwell in unity! It is like the precious oil on the head, running down on the beard, on the beard of Aaron, running down on the collar of his robes! It is like the dew of Hermon, which falls on the mountains of Zion! For there the LORD has commanded the blessing, life forevermore.
– Psalm 133:1-3

The ANOINTING

Father, in the name of Jesus, thank You for the fellowship we have with like-Spirited people. It refreshes us, challenges us, and moves us forward. Thank You for manifesting Your oil among Your people and for displaying Your truths to us as we gather in Your great name.

40

I esteem and value the
anointing of God's Spirit!

*Precious treasure and oil are
in a wise man's dwelling, but
a foolish man devours it.*
– Proverbs 21:20

The ANOINTING

Father, in the name of Jesus, I invite You today to lift me higher. Lift me into every vision that concerns me. I want to see what You are prophetically revealing as You anoint my eyes. Give me clarity to see and a willing spirit to receive this day.

41

I am determined to receive every
benefit of the anointing!

Your anointing oils are fragrant;
your name is oil poured out;
therefore virgins love you.
– Song of Solomon 1:3

The ANOINTING

Father, in the name of Jesus, thank You for filling me more and more with the knowledge of Your glorious anointing. I love the fragrance of Your anointing and the greatness of Your name. It is to me as flowing oil pouring forth. And, yes, in return, I love You more and more!

42

I am living in powerful breakthrough because of God's anointing!

And in that day his burden will depart from your shoulder, and his yoke from your neck; and the yoke will be broken because of the fat [the anointing].
– Isaiah 10:27

The ANOINTING

Father, in the name of Jesus, when I am burdened for any reason, You are there to lift that burden from my shoulders. When I feel the enemy attempting to place any yoke upon my neck, You remove it. Yes, You break that yoke because of the anointing, and You set me free. You work all things together for my good, so that I can continue to declare Your mighty works.

43

I have been anointed to bring
Good News wherever I go!

*The Spirit of the LORD GOD is upon
me, because the LORD has anointed me
to bring good news, ... to bind up the
brokenhearted, to proclaim liberty to
the captives, to proclaim the year of
the LORD's favor, ... to comfort all who
mourn; ... that he may be glorified.*
– Isaiah 61:1-3

The ANOINTING

Father, in the name of Jesus, I dedicate my lips this day to the proclamation of Your Good News. No more complaining, no more fault finding, no more negative thinking and speaking. I will believe Your promises and proclaim them everywhere I go, to everyone I meet along my path.

44

I am ready to make any necessary
sacrifice to maintain the anointing
of God's Spirit on my life!

*I ate no delicacies, no meat or wine
entered my mouth, nor did I anoint
myself at all, for the full three weeks.*
– Daniel 10:3

The ANOINTING

Father, in the name of Jesus, Your ways are always best. Maintaining the touch of Your anointing upon my life is more important to me than anything or anyone else. Continue to fill me to overflowing, and I will do Your will and seek to extend Your Kingdom on every hand.

45

I am a lover of God!

For I desire steadfast love and not sacrifice, the knowledge of God rather than burnt offerings.
– Hosea 6:6

The Anointing

Father, in the name of Jesus, I acknowledge Your desire for my life: a steadfast love and the knowledge of You. This is not bondage, but freedom. Teach me to cherish every word that comes forth from Your lips, for each one leads me higher, Help me to live my life in perfect obedience to Your Spirit, and I know that I will increase in the power of Your anointing.

46

I am anointed to dream and prophesy!

And it shall come to pass afterward, that I will pour out my Spirit on all flesh; your sons and your daughters shall prophesy, your old men shall dream dreams, and your young men shall see visions.
– Joel 2:28

The ANOINTING

Father, in the name of Jesus, thank You for the dreams and visions that illuminate my life, and thank You for using me to release Your prophetic oracles! I will speak as You anoint my mind and my mouth. Let an even greater anointing come upon me, so that I might have greater illumination and become a greater blessing to all those around me.

47

I am determined not to miss
the day of my visitation!

*You shall sow, but not reap; you
shall tread olives, but not anoint
yourselves with oil; you shall
tread grapes, but not drink wine.*
– Micah 6:15

The ANOINTING

Father, in the name of Jesus, I don't want to miss any of the blessings and favor You have prepared for my life. Let me reap fully where I have sown. Let me benefit always from the oil of Your anointing power in every situation. Let me constantly drink the sweet wine of Your Holy Spirit until I am more than satisfied.

48

I am connected to the Source
of all goodness!

*The LORD is good, a stronghold
in the day of trouble; he knows
those who take refuge in him.*
– Nahum 1:7

The ANOINTING

Father, in the name of Jesus, I recognize Your goodness and thank You that You know those who take refuge in You. You are my Refuge, and I will not fear any enemy that may attack me or try to destroy my soul. None can stand against me, for none can stand against You! Therefore, nothing shall hinder my advance, and no enemy shall stand against me, for You are my God. Be exalted in and through my life.

I choose to live by the Spirit!

Then he said to me, "This is the word of the Lord to Zerubbabel: 'Not by might, nor by power, but by my Spirit,' says the Lord of hosts."
– Zechariah 4:6

The
ANOINTING

Father, in the name of Jesus, You know well the struggles of my life. When I give You full rein, I am able to overcome, but when I try to do things in my own strength, I fail utterly. This has taught me that I must rely more and more upon Your Spirit, even in the small matters of daily life. I am so limited, and You are so unlimited. As I allow You to cloak me in Your Spirit, I am able to take on divine attributes and to actually do Your works. May all the glory be unto Your name!

50

I am powerfully anointed
from head to toe!

But when you fast, anoint your
head and wash your face.
– Matthew 6:17

The ANOINTING

Father, in the name of Jesus, You are my Life, and without You I am nothing. This causes me to do whatever I must to maintain Your touch upon my life. I have never considered this to be sacrifice or hardship. To the contrary, it is joy for me, knowing that the end result will be to my benefit. You fill me through and through.

51

I am anointed with godly wisdom
to discern the times and seasons!

*Then the kingdom of heaven will be
like ten virgins who took their lamps
and went to meet the bridegroom. Five
of them were foolish, and five were
wise. For when the foolish took their
lamps, they took no oil with them, but
the wise took flasks of oil with their
lamps. As the bridegroom was delayed,
they all became drowsy and slept.*
– Matthew 25:1-5

The ANOINTING

Father, in the name of Jesus, I delight in Your presence, I love to worship You, I love to sing Your praises, and I love to listen for Your words of comfort and admonition. I know that You love me, and I know that You desire to bless and prosper every aspect of my daily life. Have Your way with me this day.

52

I am anointed for
healing and deliverance!

*And they cast out many demons
and anointed with oil many who
were sick and healed them.*
– Mark 6:13

The ANOINTING

Father, in the name of Jesus, You are not only my Healer; You anoint me for the healing of others. Thank You for the privilege of honoring You in this way. I want the whole world to know how good You have been to me, and I want others to receive Your healing power demonstrated in their lives, that they, too, might know You and serve You.

53

I am anointed as a miracle worker!

The Spirit of the Lord is upon me, because he has anointed me to proclaim good news to the poor. He has sent me to proclaim liberty to the captives and recovering of sight to the blind, to set at liberty those who are oppressed, to proclaim the year of the Lord's favor.

— Luke 4:18-19

 The ANOINTING

Father, in the name of Jesus, I am a miracle worker, I am anointed to do miracles in my time, and I am walking in miracles every single day. What could be more wonderful! Help me to proclaim Your miracle-working power to others, and help me to be an example of Your miracle-working power everywhere I go, because miracles glorify You!

54

I am in unity with Christ, therefore I qualify to carry His precious anointing!

And behold, a woman of the city, who was a sinner, when she learned that he was reclining at table in the Pharisee's house, brought an alabaster flask of ointment.

– Luke 7:37

The ANOINTING

Father, in the name of Jesus, You are the Anointed One, but You have offered me a place at Your table. I am honored to accept Your invitation to be part of Your Kingdom and to be part of Your family. What greater honor could I ever hope for! Today, I, too, pour out my gift of love upon You. Be glorified in and through my life.

55

I am what I am today because of
the anointing of God's Spirit!

*And standing behind him at his feet,
weeping, she began to wet his feet
with her tears and wiped them with
the hair of her head and kissed his feet
and anointed them with the ointment.*
– Luke 7:38

 The ANOINTING

Father, in the name of Jesus, my tears of joy join those of believers past and present who have benefited from Your love. Allow me to kiss Your feet and bathe them with soothing ointment. You are worthy of every act of worship and honor. Nothing that I could spend upon You would come close to expressing my deep love and adoration. All that I am today is only because of You.

56

I praise and honor the One who
is due all praise and honor!

*You did not anoint my head
with oil, but she has anointed
my feet with ointment.*
– Luke 7:46

The ANOINTING

Father, in the name of Jesus, thank You for the privilege of praise and for the privilege of Spirit-filled worship. Before You anointed my life with Your Spirit, I was unable to express the deep longings of my soul and my deep love for You. Worship in the Spirit is such a joy. It releases me into all that You have for my life. Thank You for opening Your heavens within me, so that I can anoint You with my heavenly song.

57

I am anointed to serve God's people!

He went to him and bound up his wounds, pouring on oil and wine. Then he set him on his own animal and brought him to an inn and took care of him.
– Luke 10:34

The ANOINTING

Father, in the name of Jesus, You have placed in my heart the desire to bless others. May I do it in word and also in deed. As You have been so merciful to me, help me to be merciful to others. As You have been so generous with me, help me to be generous with others. As You have been so long-suffering with me, help me to be longsuffering with others. May the Christ in me be seen in my words and my deeds.

58

I lay down my own personal
agendas to honor God!

*Then they returned and prepared spices
and ointments. On the Sabbath they
rested according to the commandment.*
– Luke 23:56

The ANOINTING

Father, in the name of Jesus, the deepest longing of my soul is to honor You in every possible way. I honor You by setting aside time to commune with Your Spirit. I honor You by making Your Word an integral part of my daily life. I honor You by joining with other members of Your Body in times of praise, worship, and reflection. I honor You by waiting in Your Spirit, that You might show me Your will for my life and how I might bless others. Teach me new ways to honor You today.

59

My life is filled with the fragrant
perfumes of heaven!

*Mary therefore took a pound of
expensive ointment made from
pure nard, and anointed the feet
of Jesus and wiped his feet with
her hair. The house was filled with
the fragrance of the perfume.*
– John 12:3

The ANOINTING

Father, in the name of Jesus, thank You allowing me to have such heavenly experiences while still here on the earth. When I awake each morning, Your heavenly light floods my soul, and even as I sleep heaven invades my consciousness. Your angels are all around me night and day. In the darkest places and in the most desperate situations, I can sense the fragrance of Your perfume, and I am at peace.

60

I am supernaturally anointed
in every situation!

*For truly in this city there were
gathered together against your
holy servant Jesus, whom you
anointed, both Herod and Pontius
Pilate, along with the Gentiles
and the peoples of Israel.*
– Acts 4:27

The ANOINTING

Father, in the name of Jesus, I rest assured in Your presence and the knowledge that no power, whether of men or of devils, can do me harm. You, my God, have set Your holy angels about me to protect me on every hand. Therefore, I need not fear the plots against my soul. I am secure in Your loving arms.

61

I am strong and capable
because of the anointing!

*But Saul increased all the more
in strength, and confounded the
Jews who lived in Damascus by
proving that Jesus was the Christ.*
– Acts 9:22

 The ANOINTING

Father, in the name of Jesus, with every challenge I face in life, I know that You are strengthening me, empowering me, and enabling me. Therefore, I know that I will always overcome and bring You glory in the process. Help me to confound those who would oppose Your work.

62

I am anointed to do good!

*How God anointed Jesus of Nazareth
with the Holy Spirit and with power.
He went about doing good and
healing all who were oppressed by
the devil, for God was with him.*
– Acts 10:38

The ANOINTING

Father, in the name of Jesus, that same anointing that enabled Jesus to do good and to bring healing to those in need is now accompanying me. I know that this would be impossible for me in my own strength. Now, however, nothing is impossible to me, as I continue to believe. I choose to walk in the goodness of Your anointed touch upon my life.

63

I am seeing extraordinary miracles through the anointing of God's Spirit on my life!

And God was doing extraordinary miracles by the hands of Paul, so that even handkerchiefs or aprons that had touched his skin were carried away to the sick, and their diseases left them and the evil spirits came out of them.
– Acts 19:11-12

 The ANOINTING

Father, in the name of Jesus, as You anoint me, the most unusual and out-of-the-ordinary things are happening. I could do none of these things myself. In You, by You, and through You, I can do all things, anything and everything. Let everything that I do and say lift up Jesus.

64

I belong to Christ, and I am
anointed by God's Spirit!

*You, however, are not in the flesh
but in the Spirit, if in fact the Spirit
of God dwells in you. Anyone
who does not have the Spirit of
Christ does not belong to him.*
– Romans 8:9

The ANOINTING

Father, in the name of Jesus, thank You for showing me how to overcome my flesh. It is by allowing Your Spirit to dwell in me and work through me. Because I have the Spirit, I belong to You, and this anointing sets me apart from others. Use me more and more for Your eternal purposes.

65

I am determined to depend more
and more on God's abilities!

*For Christ did not send me to baptize
but to preach the gospel, and not with
words of eloquent wisdom, lest the
cross of Christ be emptied of its power.*

– 1 Corinthians 1:17

The ANOINTING

Father, in the name of Jesus, I am nothing without You. With You, the opposite is true; I can do all things through Christ who strengthens me. I will not approach the Gospel with my intellect; I will depend on Your Spirit to reveal what I should share, to guide how I present it, and to demonstrate the truthfulness of it with signs following.

66

I am anointed by Christ, and He
has put His seal on my life!

*And it is God who establishes
us with you in Christ, and has
anointed us, and who has also put
his seal on us and given us his Spirit
in our hearts as a guarantee.*
— 2 Corinthians 1:21-22

The ANOINTING

Father, in the name of Jesus, thank You for the amazing confidence You have placed in my heart through the Holy Spirit. While so many struggle to find their identity in our modern world, You have given me the full assurance that I am on the right track and that what I am doing will count for eternity. This brings me unlimited peace and calm.

67

I am the righteousness of
God in Christ Jesus!

*For our sake he made him to
be sin who knew no sin, so
that in him we might become
the righteousness of God.*
— 2 Corinthians 5:17

The ANOINTING

Father, in the name of Jesus, I do not come to You in my own righteousness but in the righteousness that is in Christ alone. Your Spirit has cleansed me. Your Spirit has empowered me. And it is through the anointing of Your Spirit that I do the same works and even greater works than Jesus did here on earth.

68

I love the ways of heaven, and
I am anointed with joy!

*But of the Son he says, "Your
throne, O God, is forever and ever,
the scepter of uprightness is the
scepter of your kingdom. You have
loved righteousness and hated
wickedness; therefore God, your God,
has anointed you with the oil of
gladness beyond your companions."*
— Hebrews 1:8-9

The ANOINTING

Father, in the name of Jesus, You have caused a complete turnaround in my life. What I once loved I now hate, and what I once hated I now love. I delight in You, in Your presence, in the moving of Your Spirit, and in Your service. The anointing makes all the difference in my life.

69

I am anointed for the healing of
the sick, the casting out of devils,
and the raising of the dead!

*Is anyone among you sick? Let him
call for the elders of the church, and
let them pray over him, anointing
him with oil in the name of the
Lord. And the prayer of faith will
save the one who is sick, and the
Lord will raise him up. And if he has
committed sins, he will be forgiven.*
– James 5:14-15

The ANOINTING

Father, in the name of Jesus, through the anointing of Your Spirit, I am ready for the miraculous call. Thank You for establishing my personal life to the point that I can now be a blessing to others. Use me for healing, for deliverance, and for the salvation of many, for Your Kingdom's sake.

70

I am dedicated to that which is eternal!

Do not love the world or the things in the world. If anyone loves the world, the love of the Father is not in him.
— 1 John 2:15

The ANOINTING

Father, in the name of Jesus, thank You for the day You spoke to me and enabled me to make that eternal decision to live for Christ. My life has never been the same since. Help me to live my life as a living testimony that radiates with the light of Your eternal Kingdom.

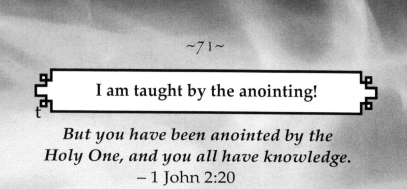

71

I am taught by the anointing!

*But you have been anointed by the
Holy One, and you all have knowledge.*
– 1 John 2:20

The ANOINTING

Father, in the name of Jesus, before You filled me with Your Spirit and taught me to listen to Your voice, I often walked as one who was blind. Now I see clearly. You daily lavish me with the knowledge and wisdom I need for every task. It is through the anointing that I gain heavenly insight into any subject! Therefore, life is so much more enjoyable as I lean on You for understanding in all things. You make me better at everything I do.

72

I rely on the Spirit of God for counsel!

But the anointing that you received from him abides in you, and you have no need that anyone should teach you. But as his anointing teaches you about everything, and is true, and is no lie— just as it has taught you, abide in him.

– 1 John 2:27

The ANOINTING

Father, in the name of Jesus, I thank You for the wise men and women You have brought into my life through the years. At the same time, I am compelled to recognize the limitations of our human wisdom. Thank You for Your Spirit. When all else fails, You are there to whisper to my heart and show me the correct way. I know I can trust You, for You never fail.

73

I know that the same Jesus
who walked on earth now lives
and works through me!

*By this we know that we abide
in him and he in us, because he
has given us of his Spirit.*
– 1 John 4:13

The ANOINTING

Father, in the name of Jesus, Your Spirit reveals to me the truth of Your abiding, and this is confirmed by the amazing signs and wonders You do in my everyday life. Most importantly, I know that I abide in You because You have given me of Your Spirit. May that abiding never diminish, but rather grow greater and greater with each passing day.

About the Author

Joshua Mills is an internationally recognized ordained minister of the Gospel, as well as a recording artist, keynote conference speaker, and author of more than thirty books and spiritual training manuals. He is well known for his unique insights into the glory realm and prophetic sound. Wherever Joshua ministers, the Word of God is confirmed by miraculous signs and wonders that testify of Jesus Christ. He is regarded as a spiritual forerunner in the Body of Christ.

Joshua and his wife Janet co-founded International Glory Ministries and have physically ministered in more than seventy-five nations on six continents. Featured together in several film documentaries and print articles, they have ministered to millions around the world through radio, television, and their weekly webcast, *Glory Bible Study*. They enjoy life with their three children—Lincoln, Liberty, and Legacy—and their puppy, Buttercup.

To contact the author about speaking invitations, other resources, and upcoming spiritual training seminars, or for prayer, please visit or email:

www.JoshuaMills.com

info@joshuamills.com

Available Audios by Joshua Mills

<u>Music</u>
- *Christmas Miracle*
- *No Limitations*
- *SpiritSpa*
- *SpiritSpa 2*
- *SpiritSpa Christmas*

<u>Soaking & Prayer</u>
- *Activating Angels In Your Life*
- *Creative Spark*
- *Experience His Glory*
- *Healing from the Psalms*

- *Opening The Portals*
- *Prayer Power*
- *Receive Your Healing*
- *Reversing The Clock*
- *You Are Blessed*

These digital audios are available for download and streaming through most online music platforms.

Become a Monthly MIRACLE WORKER
Partner with Joshua Mills and the
ministry of International Glory today!
More information available online:

www.JoshuaMills.com